EMMANUEL JOSEPH

American Crusades, The US and its Global Military Humanitarianism

Copyright © 2025 by Emmanuel Joseph

All rights reserved. No part of this publication may be reproduced, stored or transmitted in any form or by any means, electronic, mechanical, photocopying, recording, scanning, or otherwise without written permission from the publisher. It is illegal to copy this book, post it to a website, or distribute it by any other means without permission.

First edition

This book was professionally typeset on Reedsy.
Find out more at reedsy.com

Contents

1	Chapter 1: The Origins of Global Military Humanitarianism	1
2	Chapter 2: The Rise of Humanitarian Interventions	3
3	Chapter 3: The Post-9/11 Era and the War on Terror	5
4	Chapter 4: Humanitarian Interventions in Africa	7
5	Chapter 5: The Middle East and American Military...	9
6	Chapter 6: Humanitarian Interventions in Latin America	11
7	Chapter 7: The Role of International Organizations	13
8	Chapter 8: The Ethics and Legitimacy of Military...	15
9	Chapter 9: The Impact of Military Humanitarianism on US...	17
10	Chapter 10: Lessons Learned from Past Interventions	19
11	Chapter 11: The Future of American Military Humanitarianism	21
12	Chapter 12: Conclusion: Reflections on American Military...	23

1

Chapter 1: The Origins of Global Military Humanitarianism

The seeds of American global military humanitarianism were sown in the aftermath of World War II. As the dust settled, the United States found itself in a unique position of power and influence, taking on the mantle of protector of the free world. This new role was cemented by the establishment of international bodies such as the United Nations, which sought to maintain global peace and security. Over time, the US would leverage these platforms to justify and implement military interventions in the name of humanitarianism.

The Marshall Plan, aimed at rebuilding Europe, marked the beginning of a new era in US foreign policy. It showcased America's willingness to use its military and economic might to foster stability and growth in war-torn regions. However, this benevolent facade often masked underlying strategic interests. The Cold War further intensified these efforts, as the US sought to contain the spread of communism through various military and humanitarian means.

As the Cold War progressed, the US engaged in numerous military interventions under the guise of promoting democracy and human rights. These interventions, while often touted as noble endeavors, frequently led to unintended consequences and long-lasting instability. The dual nature of these actions—part humanitarian, part strategic—became a hallmark of American foreign policy.

By the end of the Cold War, the US had firmly established itself as a global enforcer of humanitarian ideals. The collapse of the Soviet Union only bolstered this position, allowing the US to act with greater impunity on the world stage. The Persian Gulf War in 1991 exemplified this new era of military humanitarianism, as the US led a coalition to liberate Kuwait from Iraqi occupation.

In the post-Cold War era, the US continued to intervene in conflicts worldwide, often citing humanitarian reasons. From Somalia to the Balkans, these interventions were driven by a mix of genuine concern for human rights and strategic interests. As the 21st century dawned, the concept of global military humanitarianism had become an integral part of the American foreign policy playbook.

2

Chapter 2: The Rise of Humanitarian Interventions

The 1990s saw a marked increase in American-led humanitarian interventions. As the sole superpower, the US felt a moral obligation to address humanitarian crises and promote global stability. This period was characterized by several high-profile interventions that highlighted the complexities and challenges of military humanitarianism.

One of the first major humanitarian interventions of the 1990s was in Somalia. In 1992, the US deployed troops as part of a United Nations mission to provide relief to a famine-stricken population. However, the operation quickly became entangled in the ongoing civil war, culminating in the infamous Battle of Mogadishu. The experience highlighted the difficulties of balancing humanitarian goals with military realities.

The Balkans presented another significant test for American military humanitarianism. In the face of ethnic cleansing and atrocities during the Bosnian War, the US eventually took a leading role in the NATO intervention. The subsequent Dayton Agreement brought an end to the conflict and underscored the potential for military intervention to achieve positive humanitarian outcomes.

In 1999, the US-led NATO intervention in Kosovo marked another milestone in the evolution of military humanitarianism. The operation aimed to stop the ethnic cleansing of Kosovar Albanians by Serbian forces. Despite controversies surrounding the legality and conduct of the intervention, it successfully ended the violence and facilitated the establishment of a UN administration in Kosovo.

Throughout these interventions, the US faced criticism for its selective approach to humanitarian crises. Critics argued that American actions were often motivated by strategic interests rather than genuine humanitarian concerns. Nevertheless, these interventions solidified the notion that the US had both the capability and responsibility to act as a global enforcer of human rights.

As the new millennium approached, the concept of humanitarian intervention had become deeply ingrained in American foreign policy. The lessons learned from the 1990s would shape the US approach to global military humanitarianism in the years to come, setting the stage for the complex and often controversial interventions of the 21st century.

3

Chapter 3: The Post-9/11 Era and the War on Terror

The terrorist attacks of September 11, 2001, marked a turning point in American foreign policy. The US response, characterized by the War on Terror, would redefine the nation's approach to global military humanitarianism. This period saw a series of interventions that combined counterterrorism objectives with humanitarian rhetoric.

The invasion of Afghanistan in 2001 was the first major operation of the War on Terror. The US-led coalition aimed to dismantle the Taliban regime and eliminate al-Qaeda's safe havens. While the primary objective was counterterrorism, the mission was also framed as a liberation effort for the Afghan people. The subsequent nation-building efforts sought to establish a stable and democratic Afghanistan, though progress was slow and fraught with challenges.

In 2003, the US launched a controversial invasion of Iraq. The stated rationale included the elimination of weapons of mass destruction, but humanitarian arguments were also prominently featured. The US promised to liberate the Iraqi people from Saddam Hussein's oppressive regime and build a democratic and prosperous Iraq. However, the invasion and its aftermath resulted in significant instability and sectarian violence, casting doubt on the effectiveness of military humanitarianism.

The War on Terror also saw American involvement in numerous other conflicts and crises worldwide. From drone strikes in Pakistan and Yemen to special operations in the Horn of Africa, the US expanded its military reach under the banner of counterterrorism and humanitarianism. These actions often blurred the lines between security objectives and humanitarian goals, leading to complex and sometimes contradictory outcomes.

Throughout the post-9/11 era, the US faced ongoing debates about the legitimacy and impact of its interventions. Critics argued that the focus on military solutions often overshadowed diplomatic and development efforts. Additionally, the prolonged nature of conflicts like those in Afghanistan and Iraq raised questions about the sustainability and long-term effectiveness of military humanitarianism.

As the War on Terror continued into the second decade of the 21st century, the US grappled with the challenges of balancing security and humanitarian objectives. The lessons learned from this period would shape future American interventions and inform the ongoing discourse on the role of military force in addressing global humanitarian crises.

4

Chapter 4: Humanitarian Interventions in Africa

Africa has been a focal point for American military humanitarianism, with numerous interventions aimed at addressing conflicts and humanitarian crises across the continent. These efforts have often been driven by a mix of altruism, strategic interests, and geopolitical considerations.

In 1993, the US intervened in Somalia to provide humanitarian aid amid a devastating famine. The mission, initially focused on relief efforts, quickly escalated into a military operation due to the complex and volatile nature of the Somali civil war. The infamous Battle of Mogadishu highlighted the challenges of conducting humanitarian interventions in conflict zones and raised questions about the effectiveness of military solutions in addressing deep-rooted issues.

The 2000s saw American involvement in various African crises, including the Darfur conflict in Sudan. In response to widespread atrocities and human rights abuses, the US supported international efforts to provide humanitarian aid and protect vulnerable populations. While direct military intervention was limited, American diplomatic and financial support played a crucial role in addressing the crisis.

In 2011, the US played a key role in the NATO intervention in Libya.

The operation aimed to protect civilians from the violent repression by the Gaddafi regime during the Libyan Civil War. While the intervention succeeded in toppling Gaddafi, it also led to prolonged instability and conflict, raising questions about the long-term consequences of military humanitarianism.

Throughout the 21st century, the US has continued to engage in military and humanitarian efforts across Africa. From counterterrorism operations in the Sahel to peacekeeping support in the Democratic Republic of Congo, American involvement has been driven by a combination of humanitarian and strategic objectives. These interventions have often been met with mixed results, highlighting the complexities and limitations of military solutions in addressing African conflicts.

The experiences in Africa have underscored the need for a comprehensive approach to humanitarian interventions. Military force alone is rarely sufficient to address the root causes of conflicts and crises. Instead, a combination of diplomatic, economic, and development efforts is essential to achieving lasting peace and stability on the continent.

5

Chapter 5: The Middle East and American Military Humanitarianism (Continued)

The experiences in the Middle East have underscored the difficulties of balancing humanitarian goals with strategic interests. The region's complex geopolitical landscape often necessitates careful navigation to avoid exacerbating existing tensions and conflicts. Despite these challenges, the US remains committed to promoting stability and human rights in the Middle East, even as the efficacy of military interventions continues to be debated.

The Arab Spring of 2011 further complicated the US approach to the Middle East. As popular uprisings swept through the region, the US faced difficult decisions about whether and how to support these movements. In some cases, such as Libya, the US opted for direct intervention, while in others, like Egypt and Syria, it pursued a mix of diplomatic and humanitarian measures. The outcomes of these actions have varied, highlighting the unpredictable nature of military humanitarianism in a volatile region.

In recent years, the US has focused on addressing the humanitarian consequences of ongoing conflicts in the Middle East. This includes providing aid to refugees and internally displaced persons, supporting reconstruction efforts, and promoting human rights and governance reforms. These initiatives aim to address the root causes of instability and create conditions for lasting peace.

The Middle East remains a focal point for American military humanitarianism, with the US continuing to balance its strategic interests with its humanitarian commitments. The region's ongoing challenges require a nuanced and multifaceted approach, combining military, diplomatic, and development efforts to achieve meaningful and sustainable outcomes.

6

Chapter 6: Humanitarian Interventions in Latin America

Latin America has also been a significant arena for American military humanitarianism, with interventions often driven by a combination of humanitarian concerns and strategic interests. The US has engaged in numerous operations aimed at addressing conflicts, promoting stability, and supporting human rights in the region.

One of the earliest examples of American military humanitarianism in Latin America was the intervention in Haiti in 1994. The US-led operation aimed to restore democratic governance and address the humanitarian crisis caused by a military coup. The intervention succeeded in restoring President Jean-Bertrand Aristide to power and stabilizing the country, though long-term challenges persisted.

In the early 2000s, the US supported efforts to address the conflict in Colombia. The US provided significant military and economic assistance to the Colombian government in its fight against insurgent groups and drug cartels. This support was framed as part of a broader effort to promote peace, stability, and development in the region. While the conflict has not been fully resolved, American involvement has played a crucial role in strengthening Colombia's capacity to address its security and humanitarian challenges.

In recent years, the US has continued to engage in humanitarian efforts in

Latin America, including disaster relief and support for refugees and migrants. For example, the US has provided aid and assistance to countries affected by natural disasters, such as the earthquake in Haiti in 2010 and hurricanes in Central America. Additionally, the US has supported efforts to address the humanitarian crisis caused by political instability and economic collapse in Venezuela, providing aid to displaced persons and neighboring countries hosting refugees.

These interventions in Latin America have highlighted the complexities and challenges of military humanitarianism. While American actions have often been motivated by genuine humanitarian concerns, they have also been influenced by strategic interests and geopolitical considerations. The experiences in the region underscore the need for a comprehensive approach that addresses the root causes of conflicts and crises while promoting long-term stability and development.

7

Chapter 7: The Role of International Organizations

International organizations have played a crucial role in shaping and supporting American military humanitarianism. These organizations provide frameworks for cooperation, legitimacy for interventions, and resources to address humanitarian crises. The US has often worked through and alongside these bodies to achieve its humanitarian objectives.

The United Nations (UN) has been a key partner in American military humanitarianism. The UN provides a platform for coordinating international responses to crises and legitimizing interventions through Security Council resolutions. The US has frequently leveraged the UN to garner support for its actions, from peacekeeping missions to humanitarian aid efforts. However, the relationship has not always been smooth, with debates over the legality and effectiveness of certain interventions.

NATO has also been an important ally in American military humanitarianism. The alliance provides a framework for collective defense and intervention, allowing the US to mobilize support from its European partners. NATO interventions, such as those in Bosnia, Kosovo, and Libya, have demonstrated the potential for coordinated military action to address humanitarian crises. However, these interventions have also raised questions about the balance between military force and diplomatic solutions.

Other international organizations, such as the European Union, the African Union, and various regional bodies, have also played important roles in supporting American military humanitarianism. These organizations provide additional resources, expertise, and legitimacy for interventions. They also facilitate cooperation and coordination among multiple actors, enhancing the overall effectiveness of humanitarian efforts.

The role of international organizations in American military humanitarianism underscores the importance of multilateralism and cooperation. While the US often takes a leading role in interventions, the support and collaboration of international partners are essential for achieving meaningful and sustainable outcomes. These partnerships help to ensure that humanitarian interventions are conducted within a broader framework of international law and norms.

8

Chapter 8: The Ethics and Legitimacy of Military Humanitarianism

The ethics and legitimacy of military humanitarianism have been subjects of ongoing debate and controversy. While the intention to alleviate suffering and protect human rights is noble, the use of military force to achieve these goals raises complex moral and legal questions.

One of the primary ethical concerns is the principle of sovereignty. Military interventions often involve violating the sovereignty of the targeted state, which can be seen as an affront to international law and order. Proponents of humanitarian intervention argue that the protection of human rights transcends state sovereignty, while critics contend that such actions can set dangerous precedents and lead to abuses of power.

The principle of just war theory also plays a significant role in the ethics of military humanitarianism. Just war theory provides criteria for determining when the use of force is morally justified, including just cause, proportionality, and the likelihood of success. Humanitarian interventions must be carefully evaluated against these criteria to ensure that they are conducted ethically and responsibly.

The legitimacy of military humanitarianism is further complicated by the issue of selective intervention. Critics argue that the US and other powerful nations often intervene in some crises while ignoring others, based on strategic interests rather than humanitarian needs. This selective approach can undermine the credibility and legitimacy of military humanitarianism as a whole.

The potential for unintended consequences is another significant ethical concern. Military interventions, even those with the best intentions, can lead to civilian casualties, displacement, and prolonged instability. These outcomes raise questions about the morality and effectiveness of using military force to achieve humanitarian goals.

Despite these challenges, the concept of military humanitarianism remains an important tool in the international community's efforts to address crises and protect human rights. The key to ethical and legitimate interventions lies in careful planning, multilateral cooperation, and a commitment to minimizing harm and maximizing positive outcomes.

9

Chapter 9: The Impact of Military Humanitarianism on US Foreign Policy

The practice of military humanitarianism has had a profound impact on US foreign policy, shaping the nation's approach to global engagement and its role in the international community. Over the decades, the concept has evolved, influencing the strategies and priorities of American policymakers.

Military humanitarianism has reinforced the idea of the US as a global leader and enforcer of human rights. This self-perception has driven American foreign policy decisions, often leading to interventions aimed at promoting stability and addressing humanitarian crises. However, this role has also placed significant burdens on the US, requiring substantial resources and political capital.

The frequent use of military force in humanitarian interventions has also shaped the US military's structure and capabilities. The armed forces have developed specialized units and doctrines for conducting complex operations that combine combat, peacekeeping, and humanitarian aid. These capabilities have enabled the US to respond swiftly and effectively to crises but have also led to debates about the militarization of humanitarian efforts.

The practice of military humanitarianism has influenced America's relationships with its allies and partners. The US has often relied on the support and cooperation of other nations and international organizations to carry out interventions. These partnerships have strengthened America's global alliances but have also exposed tensions and disagreements over the legitimacy and effectiveness of certain actions.

At the same time, military humanitarianism has generated significant criticism and controversy, both domestically and internationally. Debates over the morality, legality, and impact of interventions have shaped public opinion and influenced political discourse. These debates have led to calls for greater accountability, transparency, and oversight in the conduct of humanitarian interventions.

The impact of military humanitarianism on US foreign policy is multifaceted, reflecting the complexities and challenges of balancing humanitarian goals with strategic interests. As the US continues to navigate the evolving global landscape, the lessons learned from past interventions will inform future approaches to addressing humanitarian crises and promoting stability.

10

Chapter 10: Lessons Learned from Past Interventions

The history of American military humanitarianism offers valuable lessons for future interventions. By examining past successes and failures, policymakers can develop more effective strategies for addressing humanitarian crises and promoting global stability.

One key lesson is the importance of clear objectives and realistic expectations. Interventions must be guided by well-defined goals and a thorough understanding of the context and challenges. Unrealistic expectations can lead to mission creep, prolonged engagements, and unintended consequences.

Another lesson is the need for comprehensive and integrated approaches. Military force alone is rarely sufficient to address complex humanitarian crises. Successful interventions require a combination of diplomatic, economic, and development efforts, as well as coordination with international partners and local actors.

The importance of multilateral cooperation is another critical lesson. Interventions conducted within a framework of international cooperation and legitimacy are more likely to achieve positive outcomes. Engaging with international organizations, regional bodies, and other nations can enhance the effectiveness and credibility of humanitarian efforts.

The experiences of past interventions also highlight the need for accountability and oversight. Transparent decision-making processes, clear lines of authority, and mechanisms for evaluating and learning from interventions are essential for ensuring ethical and effective actions.

Finally, the lessons of military humanitarianism emphasize the importance of addressing the root causes of conflicts. Long-term stability and peace require addressing underlying issues such as poverty, political oppression, and social inequality. Interventions that focus solely on immediate humanitarian needs without addressing these deeper issues are unlikely to achieve lasting success.

11

Chapter 11: The Future of American Military Humanitarianism

As the world continues to evolve, so too will the practice of American military humanitarianism. The changing geopolitical landscape, emerging threats, and evolving norms and values will shape the future of US interventions in humanitarian crises.

One key trend is the increasing importance of technology in humanitarian interventions. Advances in areas such as drone technology, cyber capabilities, and artificial intelligence offer new tools for addressing humanitarian challenges. These technologies can enhance the efficiency and effectiveness of interventions, but they also raise new ethical and legal questions that must be carefully considered.

Another trend is the growing emphasis on multilateralism and international cooperation. As global challenges become more interconnected, the US will need to work closely with international partners to address humanitarian crises. This includes engaging with international organizations, regional bodies, and other nations to coordinate responses and share resources.

The future of American military humanitarianism will also be shaped by the ongoing debates about the legitimacy and effectiveness of interventions. As the US continues to learn from past experiences, it will need to develop more nuanced and comprehensive approaches that balance humanitarian goals with strategic interests. This includes placing greater emphasis on diplomatic and development efforts, as well as ensuring that interventions are conducted ethically and responsibly.

Finally, the future of American military humanitarianism will be influenced by the changing global power dynamics. The rise of other global powers, such as China and Russia, will present new challenges and opportunities for US interventions. The US will need to navigate these shifting dynamics carefully, balancing its humanitarian commitments with its strategic interests.

In summary, the future of American military humanitarianism will be shaped by a combination of technological advancements, multilateral cooperation, evolving norms and values, and changing global power dynamics. As the US continues to address humanitarian crises worldwide, it will need to adapt and innovate to ensure that its interventions are effective, ethical, and sustainable.

12

Chapter 12: Conclusion: Reflections on American Military Humanitarianism

The history of American military humanitarianism is a complex and multifaceted story, marked by successes, failures, and ongoing challenges. From the aftermath of World War II to the present day, the US has played a significant role in addressing humanitarian crises worldwide, often combining military force with diplomatic and development efforts.

Throughout this history, the US has faced numerous ethical, legal, and practical dilemmas. The principles of sovereignty, just war theory, and multilateralism have all played crucial roles in shaping the legitimacy and effectiveness of interventions. The selective nature of interventions and the potential for unintended consequences have further complicated the practice of military humanitarianism.

Despite these challenges, American military humanitarianism has also achieved notable successes. Interventions in places like Bosnia, Kosovo, and Haiti have demonstrated the potential for military force to achieve positive humanitarian outcomes. These successes underscore the importance of clear objectives, comprehensive approaches, and international cooperation.

Looking to the future, the US will need to continue learning from past experiences and adapting its strategies to address emerging challenges. The increasing importance of technology, the need for multilateral cooperation, and the shifting global power dynamics will all shape the future of American military humanitarianism. By developing more nuanced and comprehensive approaches, the US can continue to play a vital role in promoting stability and protecting human rights worldwide.

In conclusion, American military humanitarianism is a testament to the nation's enduring commitment to addressing global challenges and promoting human rights. While the practice is fraught with complexities and controversies, it remains an essential tool in the US foreign policy playbook. By embracing the lessons of the past and adapting to the demands of the future, the US can continue to make meaningful contributions to global humanitarian efforts.

American Crusades: The US and its Global Military Humanitarianism

This compelling exploration delves into the intricate and often controversial history of American military humanitarianism. From the aftermath of World War II to the present day, the United States has repeatedly positioned itself as a global enforcer of human rights and democracy. However, these noble endeavors often intertwine with strategic interests and geopolitical considerations, leading to complex and sometimes contradictory outcomes.

The book covers key periods and events, including the Cold War, the interventions in Somalia and the Balkans, the post-9/11 era and the War on Terror, and more recent efforts in Africa, the Middle East, and Latin America. It examines the role of international organizations, the ethics and legitimacy of military interventions, and the impact of these actions on US foreign policy.

Through a detailed analysis of past interventions, the book highlights valuable lessons for future humanitarian efforts. It emphasizes the need for clear objectives, comprehensive approaches, multilateral cooperation, and a commitment to addressing the root causes of conflicts. As the US continues to navigate the evolving global landscape, this book offers a nuanced perspective on the challenges and opportunities of military humanitarianism in the 21st century.

"American Crusades: The US and its Global Military Humanitarianism" provides a thought-provoking and insightful look at the complexities of American foreign policy and the ongoing quest to balance humanitarian goals with strategic interests.

www.ingramcontent.com/pod-product-compliance
Lightning Source LLC
LaVergne TN
LVHW020742090526
838202LV00057BA/6195